INTELLIGENT DRAWING

RICO LEBRUN,

Woman in Dust Storm

From the Collection of Mr. and Mrs. Max Schott. Courtesy of the Artist

INTELLIGENT DRAWING

AN APPROACH FOR THE STUDENT

Edward L. Chase

NEW YORK   COWARD-McCANN, INC.,   *PUBLISHERS*

COPYRIGHT, 1946, BY EDWARD L. CHASE

This book is published on the same day in the Dominion of Canada by Longmans, Green & Company, Toronto.

Typography by Robert Josephy

MANUFACTURED IN THE UNITED STATES OF AMERICA

Contents 29807

I wish to thank my son, Edward T. Chase, for essential assistance he gave me in organizing and editing the main text of this book. If my ideas are clear to the reader, the credit is due in no small measure to his generous help.

E. L. C.

Illustrations

1: *By Way of Introduction*

I write this book for all who wish to learn to draw effectively and to understand the value of drawing. I do not set forth any "system." On the contrary, I must stress the danger of reliance on any system. The prime necessity is for the beginner to know that above all he must think things through himself, that he must develop his own individual creative powers with intelligence and hard work. There simply is no easy short cut.

My plan is to help the student proceed most directly with the development of his innate artistic powers, in this book through the medium of drawing. I try to answer as simply as possible both by drawings and text the questions the beginner must inevitably ask. Emphasis is placed on the value of drawing not only as an art in itself but also as the vital tool for the artist when he expresses himself on canvas. And, beyond this central aim of helping the student to draw with meaning, my design is to help develop his artistic taste and understanding.

As you see, there are drawings throughout the book. With a few exceptions they are used to illustrate in some detail the points developed in the text. Perhaps they should and will speak more clearly than the text. Keep in mind that with a few exceptions they are pertinent examples shaped by the drift of the argument and do not stand as model drawings. Besides specifically showing points in the technique of drawing, they are designed to reveal how the student might possibly observe his subject; how he might most effectively use his drawing in practice; how he could approach his subject by sketching. Just as with the text they implement, the drawings can only give direction to the student's efforts. They do not constitute a recipe to be mechanically followed.

Books and pulp magazine advertisements of the "It's Easy to Draw" variety to the contrary, it is false and ridiculous to assume that there can be any recipe or formula for learning to draw well or expressively. Yet certain basic knowledge must be acquired by the student artist, as the writer must have a vocabulary and a grammar before he can write. It is primarily here that a book like this can play its chief role. It cannot, of course, accomplish the ultimate answer, the fashioning of a creative artist. But it can introduce the student to some fundamental facts of composition, form, the place of anatomy, the constructive approach to studying action, character, drapery, the best uses of sketching, and such similar more or less "factual" information. One thing must be fully understood at this juncture. This knowledge, these fundamental "facts" I speak of, represent only the material the artist works with, similar to his more physical tools, his pencil and paper. The most adroit mastery of all these tools directed solely for exact photographic likeness of the subject must *never* be the student's goal. That ambition leads only to commonplace, artistically meaningless work. Rather, the student's effort must be through perseverance to make his factual knowledge a pliable, accessible vocabulary. The vital thing is how the artist uses this knowledge. Without it he is not likely to make really fine drawings. Fine drawing will come only after intelligent hard work and will depend not on exact representation but on how the artist has interpreted his subject, and from it created something expressive, vital, and personal.

Meantime let us understand that we are *not* concerned at the moment with ambitious finished drawings. I am instead leading you to the problems to be studied and a possible way to go about practicing. That accomplished, the completed drawing will come naturally enough.

2: *Sketching*

Goethe said: "Drawings are invaluable not only because they give in its purity the mental intention of the artist, but because they bring immediately before us the mood of his mind at the moment of creation." This is a cogent description of what we perhaps more often call the sketch. Goethe here speaks primarily of the sketch's value in terms of the appreciator. To the artist, sketching's value is immense. In fact, learning to draw is largely a matter of sketching —continually, everywhere, everything.

This means, then, that you must carry your sketch book with you at all times—and use it. In this chapter I want to speak primarily of how to go about this sketching.

We can break down free-hand draughtsmanship into three or possibly four major types. Apropos of the Goethe quotation above, there is the *quick sketch* made at the *moment of interest*. It is no more than a note, possibly for future reference, of fleeting ideas, chance discoveries, or accidental situations, of whatever happens to catch your imagination, and made without pretense of producing a perfected, finished drawing. The sketch is complete when it has recorded the interest that initiated it. Such sketching can store up your momentary inspirations from life's activities—moods, plays of light and shadow on forms, impressions of character—stored perhaps for future, more important work, to verify or recall some detail of importance. An important master has valued such sketches in these words: "The more ambitious study does not give as enduring results as those fragmentary passages that come without thought of composition. It is not the ambitous study that the artist will consult when he needs reliable help."

A second, related type of drawing consists of making various studies of some subject selected for an eventual painting or an ambitious completed drawing; or again not with the idea of leading to a completed work but rather fully to explore some chosen subject matter with the stress perhaps on action or form, emotion or drapery. This is a true search for the acquiring of knowledge. It is learning the factual mechanics of your subject. You are illustrating the "realistic" facts of your subject, learning how something works, or how it is built. This is very necessary if at times prosaic work. Without it the artist's creative efforts often will be weak, amateurish, and temperamental, marked by sentimentality rather than by expressive meaning.

There is thirdly the drawing as an end in itself. This is usually a finished drawing of a subject, such as a portrait. Probably it will have been preceded by many sketches. This completed drawing, "a final answer," should not be the early concern of the beginner.

And finally we might distinguish, as a subdivision of this drawing as an end in itself, the completed drawing that is not a direct treatment of some given subject—one which bears only an intellectual or symbolic relation to its object and embodies a highly imaginative or abstract principle. This is hardly our first problem.

To speak as I do here of the completed drawing, the drawing as final answer, end in itself, is in one important sense misleading, because no good artist ever feels wholly satisfied, although to do convincing work he must have faith in his powers. Cézanne said, "One cannot be too scrupulous or too sincere or too submissive to nature; but one should be master of one's model and certainly of one's manner of expression."

Let us look into the business of sketching as the logical start in our learning draughtsmanship.

2

The first thing I would impress upon you, the beginner, as we come to the concrete business of sketching is that you must work in complete freedom. That can mean many different things. I have already suggested one sense in which I mean this: you must be free from any notion that you should make your drawings either *correct* or *complete*. You must think of your drawing as expressive, as exploratory practice, even as intelligent play.

But sketching in freedom has its physical basis too. You must learn to draw so that you enjoy the use of your whole arm from the shoulder. That

Figure 1

means keeping your paper at a distance. If you use a drawing board, you can hold it in your lap and leaning on a table (Figure 1), or you can use it as an easel when placed on an overturned chair (Figure 2). When you use your sketch book you should draw with it in your lap. This will give you freedom to use your whole arm, and will have a second advantage: the drawing will be distant enough so that you can view the whole sheet of paper and entire drawing at all times. That is valuable.

Your grip of your pencil or crayon also has a bearing on this freedom in sketching. You should hold your crayon in your whole hand. Almost all beginners have a tendency to grip their crayon or pencil firmly, as they would

5

Figure 2

do habitually and quite naturally in writing. In drawing, such detailed accuracy and uniformity is not the goal. We are at the moment practicing—
and only practicing—for bigger things. As a matter of fact in a very short time
you will find yourself capable of controlling your hand with surprising
precision, quite as much as you will need or desire; and yet you will at the
same time enjoy freedom and range in your movements.

As a start, I suggest you make nothing but quick sketches of the simplest
subjects. You could begin by setting up on a table some simply formed
articles as still life, something with no detail of design, say a vase with an
orange, lemon, grapefruit, apple, etc., and also something of angular shape.
A piece of cardboard can be used as a background, or simply the wall. The
aim is to combine round, convex shapes with some contrasting angular shape,
say a cigarette box. You can experiment with different arrangements of these

6

articles, selecting some arrangement that interests you and that makes up a simple grouping of shadows and forms. A spotty, broken-up scattering of the articles is confusing and lacks simplicity. The arrangement should suggest some simple composition of these forms.

Now sketch. At this time the effort of importance is the building up in your drawing of a three-dimensional space which will contain these chosen articles. The exact shapes of the articles are not of first importance. Sketch in the general forms as a group quickly and freely, by sketching in the shapes of the large shadows on the objects, the shadows cast by these objects on the table surface upon which they are grouped, and the shadows cast by the objects on the background. (Figure 3.)

Figure 3

7

Figure 4

Attempt to sketch the shadows retaining the flat horizontal plane of the table and the upright surface of the wall, at the same time making the shadows on the objects build a convex, global, or square form as the case may be. (Figure 4.)

Make a number of these rough sketches. As you make the later ones you find your hand and eye are judging more easily, and your sketch taking on increasingly the true form and likeness of the still life before you. You are getting acquainted with your subject. (Figure 5.)

When you feel you have finally grasped the essential idea of form in your sketch of this still life, then try to develop the still life into a somewhat more completed work still in terms of form existing in light and shadows and not by an elaboration of the articles' details. Make every effort to have your *shadow shapes* build up this form. In this connection at first use rather colorless or light-colored articles so that in full light your shadows are in positive contrast to the forms.

When you have made many sketches for this experience with form, and of many different articles and arrangements, you will not only have a fair idea of how to think about and draw simple form, but you will also discover some development in your sense of selection.

I have suggested you begin with a simple still life. Of course you do not remain there. With your pocket sketch book you sketch everywhere at all times. Your province is quite unlimited. That is why sketching, to the imaginative and observant person, is so exciting. The sheer exercise of observing is of vital importance to your growth as an artist. This quick sketching trains you to select directly some important values of a subject,

Figure 5

Figure 6

Figure 7

10

whether a factual detail or some spiritual quality that has struck you. And also it will sharpen your awareness of people's habits and character, of the recording of interesting events about you, of the construction of landscape, the effects of lighting both indoors and out, the myriad salient aspects of life, which, ideally at least, affect the artist more intensely than the ordinary man.

Let us explore the sketching possibilities of one specific, quite prosaic example, say sketching the members of your family at home. (See Figures 6 and 7.) The person you choose to draw sits absorbed in a book. There are numerous points of interest. You must consider the subject and find what interests you most. Suppose you decide that what impresses you first is the relaxed yet at the same time concentrated attention of the person on the book. You quickly analyze to discover what lines seem most centrally to express the relaxed yet concentrated pose, and then you sketch, using these few essential lines and attempting no more than an indication of this pose. (Figures 8 and 9.)

Figure 8

11

Figure 9   Figure 10

Now you try another approach to the same subject. This time you are interested in the effect of light and shadow on the figure's form. Notice that my sketch here is wholly in terms of sheer blacks and whites, without tone values. (Figure 10.)

In the next sketch of the subject you work for form in terms of *line* and line alone. (Figure 11.)

Now, as a variation and an elaboration on the method in Figure 11, try emphasizing the contours of the form by a continuous series of lines as I have done in Figure 12. Notice how this exercise makes you particularly aware of the minor forms that flow together to make up the whole form of the figure.

12

Figure 11

13

Suppose now your model has stopped reading to relieve the intense concentration, that he moves and stretches, arm out, book in hand, head thrown back. Immediately you should note the lines of action that indicate the stretch. You sketch at once. (Figure 13.)

Thus an entire evening at home can be spent with continual intelligent observation and sketching of every person in the room. Hardly anything you do can prove more profitable to you as a draughtsman and artist. At the same time choosing these different approaches to the same subject will be a most stimulating, constructive work.

Figure 13

3: *Composition*

You have probably discovered already in your initial sketching that the problem of drawing goes beyond the depiction of the subject itself. You have found or will presently find that the effectiveness of your drawing is intimately involved with the total organization you make of all the elements that comprise the drawing. An accurate representation of some pleasant, clever arrangement still doesn't satisfy. You are now finding out about the basic creative problem of composition.

I suppose composition is most comprehensively defined as the artistic organization of your material to express most effectively what has impressed you in your subject. In drawing, composition usually consists of organizing plastic forms within a three-dimensional space. It is complicated by the fact that you must do this on a flat surface, of limited size.

The problem of composition is not quite the study in mathematics that definitions seem to suggest, because it grows inevitably from your motif, your theme, what particular thing you are trying to express about your subject. There are accordingly no iron rules about composition. It takes its own direction from the emotional impact that has first aroused you to draw your subject. Hence the artist must value highly this original, determining interest.

In this chapter we can explore some of the basic principles of composition, and the student can learn how best to go about its study. I want to show by simple, diagram-like drawings some basic methods of thinking about organization. This intention and effort to study composition need not take us away from the sort of sketching just discussed in the last chapter. There is only a shift in emphasis, a new awareness of the problem of organization.

15

Observe and sketch everywhere, but now, if you are sketching your family, try sketching and grouping two or more figures as a composition. People in a restaurant, groups of men working in the street, people in the theater, or outdoor landscape subjects all are good material for this study of composition. Of course composition does not apply only to a work of several figures. It is the aesthetically vital element of any drawing of a single figure too. But the problem of composition is more dramatically thrust upon you if you must deal with several major figures. Eventually any of your drawings will automatically reflect your skill and selective ability in composition.

In working for composition make numerous notes exploring various arrangements. Remember, as an artist you are privileged to omit or add or alter however you wish for the sake of your composition. Artistic meaning springs from this, not from the surface beauty that any subject may have itself.

The best and most fundamental advice I can give you at this early stage of your introduction to composition is that you must always have a definite direction and theme in relation to your subject matter. Your drawing must have this initial design from emotional interest on your part. Without some such direction there is no intelligent, artistic basis for a composition.

A motif or determining interest and approach will come about naturally enough. Suppose you are taking a walk through the country with your sketch book. You are suddenly struck by the scene before you—the effect of brilliant sunlight and shadow on a barn against the side of a wooded hill, a dirt road separating the barn from a white house. The scene or motif has hit you with compelling emotional force. This sunlight and shadow effect must now be your *primary direction* and approach for your drawing or eventual painting. You must hold to this direction. Analyze what has impressed you; make sketches trying simply to record the elements of first importance. These you might call your basic notes—to record the scene. I suggest you go on working out a number of very rough research sketches trying to discover what organization of your material will make the best composition. Here you must rearrange over and over. But don't lose sight of your first dominant interest and mood, in this case the sunlight and shadow; if you stray from that you can easily get lost, and your final drawing will lack the point and vividness essential to convincing direction. (See Figure 14 as one illustrating this sunlit effect and motif.)

16

Figure 14

Figure 15

Figure 16

The same farm motif on a rainy, hazy day might impress you by the effect it gives of being made up of a series of receding planes. Figure 15 should show you what I mean by this.

On a really gray day when there are no definite shadows let us suppose quite logically that this same motif has now struck you by the way it builds up into one moving coherent mass of forms. (See Figure 16.)

It may be that you intend to paint this motif. In that case besides your organizational sketches in black and white you will want to make some color sketches. These together with your other sketches should equip you to make your final painting in your studio. Occasionally you may find it valuable to revisit the scene at the same time on the same kind of day to refresh your memory or revive your emotional interest.

2

I think after describing this typical development of subject material you begin now to see what is meant by the approach, the primary direction to your motif and composition. I would like to come to grips with the problem from another, more systematic and technical direction. Our example of the farm motif as developed in terms of planes takes us rather logically to what I want to do next: namely to outline with diagram illustration several fundamental methods for internal organization of your drawings. You must understand that these sketches illustrate in highly exaggerated style very rudimentary, generalized principles for organization of three-dimensional form and space. If any one of these methods alone were to be adopted in literal fashion in your drawing it might make for considerable monotony.

In the first illustration (Figure 17) the aim is to create a composition that will have great depth and space by means of rolling, rhythmic lines and forms which carry your eye back through the space and always within the

Figure 17

Figure 18

Figure 19

confines of the composition. There is actually no linear perspective employed to create this sense of depth. It is achieved by the interrelations of the forms themselves.

This raises a basic point about composition that has not been mentioned before: the fact that effective composition must hold one's interest within the picture's limits and attract it in logical movements to the important elements. Composition that allows the interest to slide out from the picture edges because of lack of any compelling forms or lines to hold the eye makes for a weak, unbalanced composition.

Let us go on to another basic manner of composition. In this sketch (Figure 18), by means of overlapping planes there is created the movement of three-dimensional form through space. Notice that this effect does not depend on perspective or diminishing in size. In fact the forms can be increased in size as they go back in depth.

In Figure 19 solid volumes of form move through space, with one volume moving into relation with another and then returning on the opposite side. Note here particularly how this keeps the interest moving firmly within the allotted space. In a sense, one's eye enjoys the feeling of anticipation in being thus attracted through the composition.

Three-dimensional form can be created through a segmented or broken line as opposed to the continuous line of Figure 17. Figure 20 illustrates this.

In Figure 21 I give another example of how space might be created, the sense of three-dimensional form and space by simple geometric elements, planes, and volumes.

Finally in Figure 22 is illustrated the vanishing-point theory or funnel type perspective, a conventional device which, while it leads the interest back into space, often has a tendency to restrict your attention rigidly to the vanishing distance of the picture.

Of course there is no limit to the way you can create compositions expressing three-dimensional form and design. These diagrams should be suggested to you as a student. But don't assume that these are Five Basic Ways.

One practice that can be of enormous benefit to you in this matter of composition is for you to study the compositions of the masters. Analyze their basic organization. Take for example Cézanne's famous "Still Life with Apples." Without going into its color subtleties, which are of great importance to the artist's creative direction, we can see how he has created movement.

Figure 20

Figure 21

22

Figure 22

Through direction of co-ordinating planes he has achieved depth of space. At the same time the interest is held within the boundaries of the picture: it moves within the composition. Cézanne has also held together the whole with a strong framework of upright forms and dominating lines—the so-called architectural framework. Even when we reduce the composition to sheer black and white areas we find the basic areas of black, white, and gray tones are in each case firmly organized into patterns of their own, graded by moving color, planes, and tones from the corners to converge around the center of the picture. There is no monotony of form, pattern, or color in this composition, only intelligent, vital organization. It shows true artistic intelligence and positive direction in Cézanne's efforts to organize the motif. (See Figures 23 and 24.)

By all means, see all the fine work you can in the various exhibitions, museums, and good art books. Contact with any of the arts, for that matter, will help you to grow as an artist because your own imagination will be awakened to the richness and variety of life in the world about you.

23

Figure 23

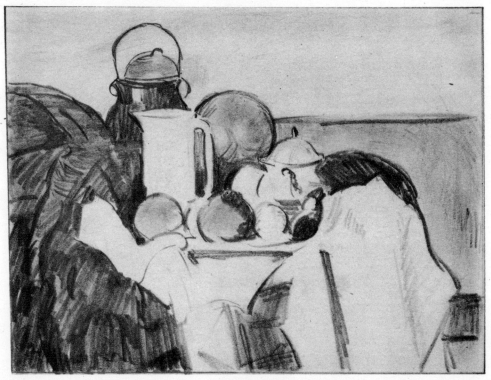

Figure 24

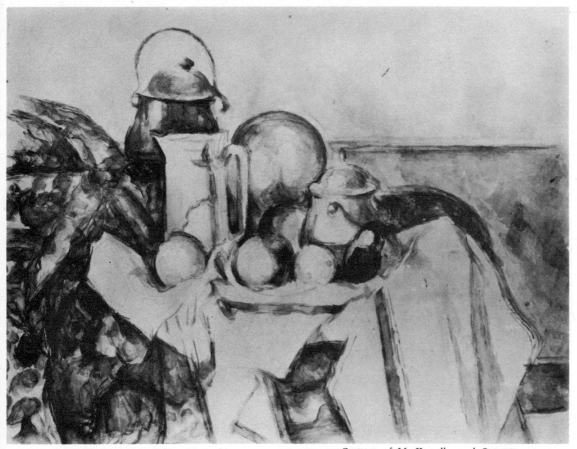

CÉZANNE, *Still Life with Apples*

3

Before we finish discussing some of these fundamental aspects of composition we ought to consider practicing composition with the use of a human model, both because no form is more interesting to draw than the human figure and because no other object is quite so adaptable to variety in study and arrangement.

As an exercise for your ability to select and organize, make a composition of several figures in some definite surrounding setting. Try to make the different poses or action of the figures co-ordinate in some way, whether in moving forms, planes, or lines, searching at the same time for variety of shapes, silhouettes, and action of form or pose. When you have made a very rough note of what you want, have a model pose for each of your roughly sketched figures, and draw each figure from the model, who must conform to your idea of each pose. In working out this composition, try to place the figures so that as a group they seem to create a definite feeling of filling up a certain cubic or third-dimensional space. Apply some of the principles on pages 83 and 84 in drawing this group of figures. Also see the drawing by Renoir (p. 82).

Make an effort in the first instance to have your arrangement of the figures create an interesting group design. But your practice in composition will not arise here primarily. More subtly, the relation of forms to one another in the composition and the rhythm of one line to another will do much to effect this sense of a definite interrelationship among the figures. (See the illustrations of Renoir and Cézanne.) At the same time this stressing of the interrelationships of the figures will create a three-dimensional form and space, filling the picture's "space."

In this type of exercise, I have in mind the use of a nude model. That is not essential, and you may in some instances feel that having one or more of the figures partly draped or even completely dressed will help your composition.

Many times you will become particularly interested in one or another of the single poses your model has taken. It is good for you in that case to make a more extended, developed drawing of that particular figure on a separate piece of paper. You can use this drawing, too, as a reference drawing while you work on your group composition.

This kind of exercise in composition can be done also from old sketches in your sketch book or from previous sketches of your models. By either method—working directly from a model or from old sketches—it is stimulating study.

4: *Form and Construction*

Since drawing for the beginner is from one basic viewpoint largely a matter of constructing, I would like in this chapter to discuss composition by and large in terms of construction and form. These are all overlapping and interrelated topics. Let us see what this means.

I have in mind first, construction in its literal sense—the way an object is built, whether a tree or a human being or a battleship. For the artist this knowledge of construction proves to be immensely valuable because, far from entangling him in the sheer mechanics of his subject, it will give him freedom in his expression of form and line. It is only after he has acquired a basic knowledge of how a thing is built that he understands what holds it together as a unit and what are its possibilities of movement. It is then that he can take his own artistic liberties, confident in his knowledge of the essentials of his subject. Without such knowledge he cannot create the feeling of a solid form, the third dimension, or the movement of form through space. And so he cannot make a good composition.

To start at the start, we can understand that for the artist construction, in a primary sense, applies to form. Now for the artist the word "form" conveys meanings that should be explained. Thus as an artist I will think of any object I am drawing not as an "object" in the common sense but as a *form* in space by which I will mean that this object has for me character and existing quality in space. The object *has* "form," and as an artist I will dignify this object, if you will, by speaking of it as a form. The everyday layman quite rightly can conceive of an object as nothing more than an object. But you and I as artists cannot. It is very important in fact that we become very sensitive to the existence of form everywhere about us and that we express form in all the drawings we make.

What I want you to do in your studying at this point is to think of form as a bulk taking up a given amount of space, a body having some weight and a definite character. I am speaking here of how you should approach any subject you are to draw (say a human head), how you should conceive of it as you begin to analyze its basic construction. To stress this sense of solid bulk in your own mind think of it as a piece of clay in your hands which you are modeling into a definite form. How would you go about it? Well, you are not a sculptor, you are a draughtsman, so practice this modeling into a definite form by drawing with soft crayon, or lithograph crayon or a very soft pencil. (See Figure 25.)

One word of caution at this point. As a beginner you will probably overmodel, see and draw too much detail in your efforts to acquire form. That is natural, but begin now to simplify your masses of form and masses of design by suggesting form with a few expressive lines (Figure 25). See how the drawings of Degas and the other masters shown in the book accomplish this. As you study your subject always walk around it to observe it from every possible side. Think of it as a form not having any real edges. You must realize that form is a continuous relation of one plane meeting and carrying on to the next until the planes or surfaces have built a complete solid mass taking up a given amount of space. (See Figure 26.) But mass can also exist in space without any obvious edge, as in Figure 27.

Let us pursue this study of form and construction in terms of the simple concrete example mentioned above, the human head. You will find that your study of the human head's construction will apply in principle to almost any subject you draw. I have suggested above how to conceive of the head as you first set about analyzing your problem of construction. You must not forget that it is a solid bulk with weight, that it has grown and developed character in a co-ordinated, definite manner.

Since you are studying construction, I suggest you place your model in a light strong enough to cast definite shadows from the nose, eye sockets, etc. If possible get a block plaster cast of the human head; and, if you can, have a human skull beside the model. It is even a good idea to have in addition an anatomical chart revealing the muscular anatomy of the head and figure.

Let me digress one moment for a word or two on anatomy, now that it has come up. I will not teach anatomy at all in this book. You can find

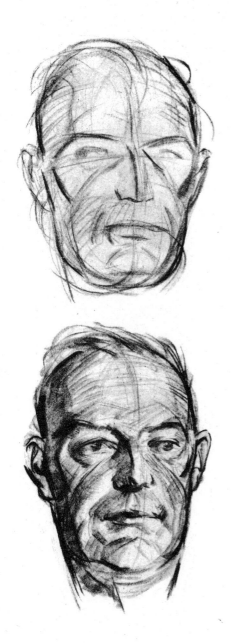
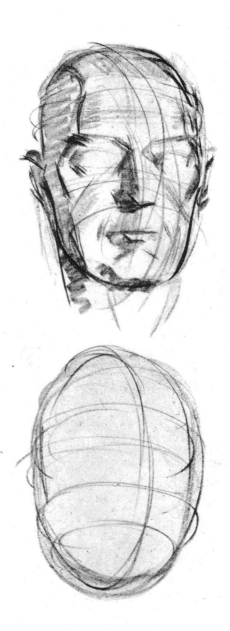

Figure 25

29

Figure 26   Figure 27

books specializing on anatomy and charts galore, and can work from them.
I suggest you study parts of the figure at a time and see how their anatomical
construction affects the form of the human figure in varying lights and positions. Also it is good practice to take some of the studies you have drawn
of figures in action and from your anatomical chart try to draw in, very correctly, the *muscles* and *skeleton* of the figures. This will help you to realize that
your shadows, halftones, highlights, and the shapes and sizes of the planes
that make up the forms are all logically caused by the underlying bones and
muscles. This is important knowledge for convincing figure drawing; but
my grave warning is that you do not become enslaved by this anatomical

30

learning with the result that all your drawings look as if they were illustrating your factual knowledge of anatomy. It is valuable to have the knowledge as a tool. Don't get lost in it.

Let us go on with the head. You have put your model under a strong light, and since you are studying construction, you have a chart or a skull or both by you. Now sketch in a few lines indicating the general form of the head. Draw in the sides of the head, top and bottom, indicating very sketchily the eye sockets, the brow, the cheek bones, nose, mouth, ears, and the jaw from ears to chin to reveal its relation to the back of the head. (See Figures 25 and 28.) Always keep in mind that you are also creating a bulky form.

Now indicate where the various muscles attach to the bone of the face. This stressing of the muscular construction will help you to work out the shadow shapes on the head which in turn will bring out the forms that make the head solid. Concentrate on your light, shadows, and shapes at this point. Before you refine them be sure your general construction is basically correct. Your block plaster cast of a head will help you here to sketch in the most obvious *planes* of the head.

As you begin to develop your shadows, observe particularly where the bone comes to the skin and disappears again under muscle or flesh. You will be surprised at the multiplicity and variety of forms caused by bone and flesh and muscle, by the eye ball, the teeth, the ears, the lips. Notice how there is a subtle contour to these forms and how they move from one into another. It is your job to make all of these fit together to create the whole solid mass of the head.

Figure 28

31

You are studying construction, so make drawings of the head from every angle until you are thoroughly acquainted with all its parts and positions. In addition, make separate studies of the various parts, the eyes, mouth, ears, etc. When you have done this you will have acquired a knowledge of the head's construction that will make any portrait work of the head vastly simpler for you. And this method of studying the head can and should be applied to all manner of poses and positions of the human figure.

2

All this study of constructions is preparation; it is not the way you would actually approach drawing a portrait of someone. With it securely behind you, however, you would be in a good position to make a portrait composition. We might finish what we have started and see what a portrait of a person would entail.

For one thing, since you are doing a portrait of an individual, be alert for the *distinguishing* characteristics of the head, what makes the individual a distinctive personality. Take your time studying the model before you draw because unless you grasp his essential character you will not get a real likeness. In fact an accurate copy of the features on paper will not make a portrait, for it will inevitably lack character and personality.

Begin, as usual, with a number of rough sketch notes, seeking out the general character of the head—whether long and narrow, elliptical like an egg, tending to be round or square, etc. Make these rough sketches from all sides. You will soon have a fairly good idea of the type of head you are dealing with. (See Figure 29 for illustrations of head types.)

Having studied your subject thus from all sides, next determine what position is most interesting to you and most characteristic of your subject. You should then pose him accordingly under a positive strong light from one direction, since such lighting emphasizes the form of his features, simplifying your analysis of character. Deciding the subject's position in the composition is very important in portrait composition and deserves more elaboration. You are expressing the character of a living, distinctive human being who thinks and feels. And it is primarily in the face that this individual life is expressed. Therefore your composition must be so designed that the face is the dominating

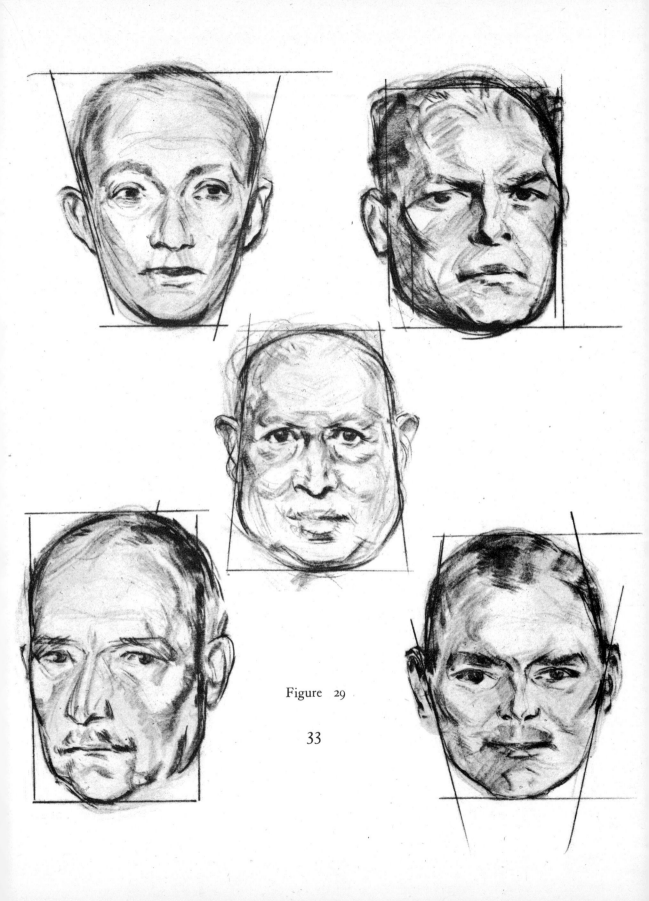

Figure 29

33

Figure 30   Figure 31

center of interest. Be sure that all line directions lead to this center. (See Figure 30.)

It may seem to you that a portrait of head or a bust does not allow much variation in the overall design. In fact it is just this relative limitation of possibilities that makes it important that you avoid any monotony in your composition. This is difficult too, for while you want to strive for variety, movement, and interest in the composition, still you must not detract from the center of interest, the head and face.

I suggest that at least you should not place the head in the center of the picture surface. This makes for monotony because the head is equidistant from the picture's frame, making a static pattern of forms allowing no suggestion of movement. In the same connection, do not have your subject face directly out from the picture but, if you wish a straight-on view of the face, have the shoulders turned to one side (Figure 31) and, if your study includes the whole torso or a suggestion of most of it, be sure to utilize the arms and hands in the making of an interesting design. Again, the contrasting *light* and *dark* patterns of, say, the face and hair or shoulders are vital elements in your composition in addition to the element of line and form.

You have made sketches studying the general type of character of the head. Make other ones exploring the placing of the subject and determining the composition. This accomplished, and now quite familiar with the individual's personality before you, you can go ahead drawing in the features

34

of the head. Develop all the parts of the head and composition together; never attempt finishing any one part separately. You must build up the whole head as the solid form it is, tying in all the elements into the organic unity they comprise in life. At every stage in your work be sure you have the true character of the personality you are drawing so that your work grows from his special character—in other words don't think you can successfully impose the true likeness as a final step. And it will be above all in the eyes and around the mouth that you will discover the inner personality of your subject, which you must at all times search to understand and realize the likeness of the individual.

3

By and large I have talked quite a bit about construction, form, and composition in drawing. But before I leave the subject, I want to say something about construction and form and composition in landscape, also the drawing of trees. (See Figures 32, 33, 34, 35.) This allows us to discuss the topic in terms of subject matter radically in contrast to the subject of the human being—although, as I have said, the same principles in large measure apply to everything you draw. As a teacher, I know that few students realize that it is just as difficult and important to draw any part of a landscape, such as a tree, as it is to draw a portrait of a human being. It requires just as much hard study, for it demands the same thorough understanding of the construction and anatomy of all the variety of forms that make up nature. In this study, drawing is an important medium. To paint landscape well one must first be able to draw it well. All this hard study is well rewarded: few subjects have struck man's imagination and sense of beauty more vividly than the aspects of nature that have conventionally comprised the subject matter of landscape painting.

If drawing by some system of rules was ridiculous elsewhere, it is doubly so when one turns to landscape. The forms, growths, colors, lights, textures, lines, and moods in nature are infinite. Still, when you come to study construction here, you again should think of your landscape as one large solid form existing in a great space of air. It is a great form made up of many forms rolling in contours into one another: vast stretches of swelling ground, great forms of clouds in airy space—the whole existing in direct sunlight, or

Figure 32

Sycamores

the diffused light of cloudy days, or in moonlight. This lighting is of vital significance because it largely controls nature's mood, a thing that can change each hour of the day out-of-doors and affects things animate and inanimate, including buildings, animals, and people. In drawing landscape particularly, constructing your composition will call for much elimination of detail and a keen sense of selection. We have already gone into that in some detail in Chapter 3 when we discussed landscape composition. Here I would stress the point that this eliminating and altering that goes into landscape or outdoor composition becomes an intelligent process only after a firm understanding of

36

the construction of the individual forms, such as trees, hills, clouds, which make up your landscape.

The tree as a form in landscape is a good form for us to consider a moment as a landscape artist might, since it differs so radically from the human being which we have treated to a degree. As a subject it is equally as "difficult" to draw as the human figure and requires just as much study of its construction. Trees vary tremendously too; you must understand the various types, how their leaves differ in detail, and how they appear as masses; and how trees look together in a group.

Poets and theorists on the nature of art have remarked that the artist often seems to look upon the world with the same naïve freshness of vision as the child. So as a student of trees it is important to remember with something of this fundamental wonder that a tree grows out of the ground and is held firm to the ground by roots that extend through the ground; but that at the

Figure 33

Figure 34

same time it is pliable in the wind, and its gradual growth is a graceful thing unless this growth has been interfered with.

It is important that you think of the tree as a three-dimensional form, yet not a solid bulk; that the air, light, birds can pass freely through its form of leaves and branches. It is usually a perpendicular, pliable form, in the summer quite controlled in this form by the particular growth of its leaves. (Be careful to observe the umbrella-like growth of the clusters of leaves in their relation to the branches that they are growing over and are held up by. The sky "holes" through the trees must be patterned by the growth of the trunk and branches, and also by the leaf clusters. The sky holes will help build your tree growth and construction.) After the leaves have fallen, go out and make careful studies of the different types of growth of trees in your part of the country. You can study then the way the branches grow out of the trunk of each species—apple; oak; maple, hard and soft; chestnut; elm; pine; and many others—how far they extend in growth, how their leaf carrying twigs cover them, and a score of such intimate observations. Continual study and sketching like this will preclude your making the dreary mistakes of so many landscape students who seem invariably either to make their trees stubby and bushy or like long inorganic cones, instead of slowly growing forms of character and beauty.

Together with your study of tree construction make studies of all formations and constructions out-of-doors. Make drawings in attempt to create space and great depth of form and movement. Watch and record intelligently the effect of the moods of nature on the landscape and on the sky—the effect wind, rain, snow, cold, heat, and light have on the whole outside world. These will make your drawings truly outdoor landscape, alive and expressive of the time and season.

Figure 35

39

5: *Action—Drapery*

One factor of the greatest importance has not yet entered into our discussion of drawing. That factor is action or the effect of movement in the subject matter. With our stress on practicing construction and our concern with the portrait of a human head the dynamic aspect of the human figure may seem to have been overlooked. Now I would like to point out some aspects of this problem and how you might go about studying the effects of action, shifts of weight, and gestures expressing emotion in the human figure. This must be done with a nude model.

You should begin quite simply by analyzing the basic changes in the human figure caused by. varying shifts of weight. As example first have your model take a simple standing pose, quite relaxed, with heels together, weight evenly distributed on both feet, arms hanging relaxed, facing straight ahead, no twist in the head or body. Study this pose, making notes of the relation of each side to the other, in lines, as indicated (Figure 36). Make drawings that you think will help you most in understanding the specific effects on the figure of the evenly distributed weight.

Next have the model shift the entire weight to one foot and make sketches studying carefully the effect this weight shift has on the entire figure from head to foot. Note that this shift of weight to one foot has caused the other leg to relax, with a dropping down of the hip and an effect of stretch and pull on that side. Whereas on the side that the weight has been shifted to the hip has been pushed up and the side folded and shortened, with this action causing a bend in the body indicated partly by the position of the spinal column and resulting in even a slight change in the shoulders (Figure 37).

40

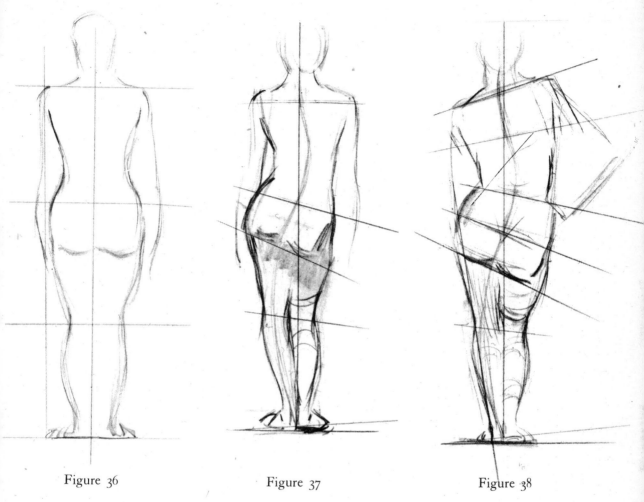

Figure 36   Figure 37   Figure 38

Now have the model put her hand on her hip on the relaxed side and make another sketch. You will notice that this move has caused still more of a stretch between the shoulder and hip. I suggest that you make drawings and diagrams from the front, back, and side, in each instance analyzing the reasons for the changes in the figure (Figures 38 and 39). You must consider that, despite these various shifts in weight causing relatively radical changes in the model's pose, the distribution of weight has so taken place that the whole figure is always balanced. You must strive to express this balance. I suggest that you next have your model, while maintaining the same stance of all her weight on one foot, twist her body and head to the "folded" side

41

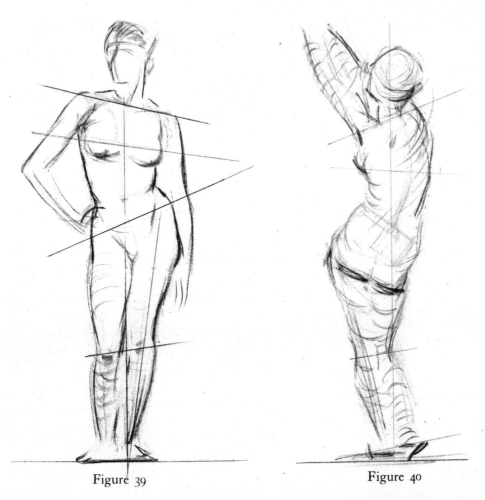

Figure 39   Figure 40

and reach up with both arms above her head and out to the same side (Figure 40). You will observe that in this action a rotating motion and twist is imparted to every part of the body from the feet up. Again you must analyze this carefully, remarking all the changes in the figure. And again you note that this extreme distribution of weight still allows a balance in the figure so that the model can remain standing.

Studying in this fashion is excellent for your drawing; do it for many hours at scattered times with changes in pose for each sketch until you feel that you could make a quick observation of your model's pose, turn your back and from memory make an intelligent, successful action sketch. This is a fairly sure test of your understanding of what action does to the figure. Eventually I would like you to shorten the time taken for these sketches until

42

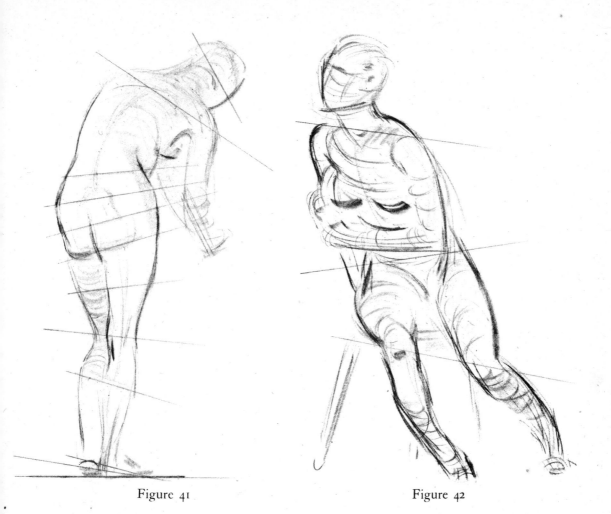

Figure 41   Figure 42

you can make drawings of the general action and form in three to five minutes, or less. Of course there is no limit to the number of action poses your model can take—and you can contribute variety by continuing these studies from different sides of the figure. (See Figures 41 and 42.)

So far we have been dealing with sustained poses implying action in the primary sense of shift in weight. This is an essential if largely preparatory study to drawing forms in actual motion and expressing emotional states through artistic drawing of gestures. To put it another way, the type of drawing outlined above is the prelude to the real thing, to expressing the vital, emotional, dynamic human figure as it moves and as it expresses its inner life through its movements and gestures. Of course this cannot in any sense be a mechanical process; you are on your own, seeking to work out what are

43

the most expressive lines, to catch the dramatic element in the moving form before you, the underlying emotional pressure behind the gesture, whether fear, joy, temper, excitement, boredom, or whatever it may be. In this kind of drawing of course your only method is to watch people in action and their gestures. You then make quick mental notes and attempt to record the note in pencil, seeking to hit upon just those lines and forms that catch the action or emotional gesture. Here is a real function of the pocket sketch book. With your earlier studies of your model in action poses thoroughly absorbed, you will find that now you are able to make these real action drawings convincing and artistically intelligent. I suggest as a very important study that you take these same poses, put clothes on the model, and study the effect of the action on the clothes and drapery. It might be very enlightening to draw right over the nude drawings suggesting the stress and strain caused by the action.

2

In the foregoing we have discussed one, and the main, factor that modifies the human form (or for that matter any moving form)—namely *action*. There is another modifying factor, quite fundamental, that I want to say a few words about here. I have in mind drapery, by which I mean the clothes people wear or the materials that may cover any object you happen to draw. Since there will be drapery in many subjects you will draw or paint, and because it constitutes a difficult and very important element in your work, you must master its effects thoroughly. It decisively affects form and, reciprocally of course, takes its own character from the underlying form. (See Figures 43 and 44.) It can be a major element in your expression of form, rhythm, action, and in the overall success of your compositions. Let me try to indicate some of its characteristics pertinent to the artist and how you can approach studying drapery.

Naturally you at first consider the particular material in question, observing its texture, whether it is soft, thick, and pliable, or thin, crisp, and stiff. This quality and thickness of the material greatly affect the character of the drapery's reaction to the pressures of forms and actions it comes into contact with. As you draw drapery you will also notice the strain on the drapery of its own weight as it hangs from one form to another. As the layman

44

Figure 43

knows, but as you the artist must note more acutely, the behavior and softer the cloth the rounder will be the form, and the thinner the cloth the more elliptical will be the shape of the folds; crisper or stiffer cloth will be more angular as it drapes over or falls away from underlying form.

You must go about studying drapery quite directly. Drape material over all types of forms, round or square. Pin your drapery on the wall in several places to achieve a variety of forms in the folds and design of the drapery. You can have it hang draping over a table to the floor or over a chair. It does not matter just how you set it up. Experiment continually. It is occasionally a good idea, when you can, to drape a sheet or a large piece of cloth over a form that will not have to be removed for several days so that you can make a very thorough study and drawing of this same subject. Also you must make studies of clothes on the human figure, men's and women's

45

Figure 44

clothes, how they hang on the form and how they are affected by changes
of position and by action as the people walk, run, or sit down. Make studies
of the clothes of the people of your family or of the people who are around
you working. Take parts at a time, studying, for example, the effect of the
shoulder or chest on the material, or the arm at the elbow or the knee or
around the neck. (See Figures 45 and 46.) You will observe that drapery is
much fuller in form as it hangs between the points of contact or where it is
confined by pressure or weight. Note too the varying thickness or density
in the folds as the drapery falls or pulls away from the points of strain or
restriction.

Of course your first aim is to have your drapery appear to be, quite
convincingly, determined by the exact form which is underneath—it must
express this form, not appear flat or simply arbitrarily overstuffed, and irrelevant

46

to the character of the determining form (Figure 47). But more than this you should strive to use your drapery for its own contribution in making a more beautiful design, form, or action in giving an added force to the artistic meaning of the particular pose you are drawing. This will also mean selection again. Certain wrinkles or folds in your drapery will have no positive artistic value in helping your expression and these must be eliminated just as others will be stressed.

Your sense of selection can be sharpened nicely by seeing as much of the masters' work as you can. Study their texture and use of drapery.

Finally, your studies of drapery should achieve the point where a sculptor could use your drawing for reference as a model. By then you will have come to a real understanding of drapery as form. This understanding will give you greater freedom to extend your emotional values and artistic intentions.

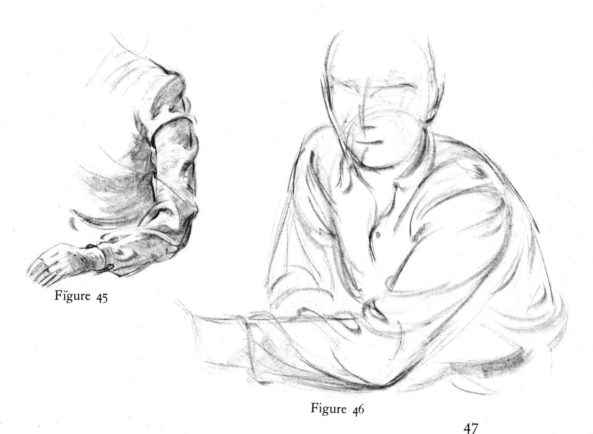

Figure 45

Figure 46

Figure 47

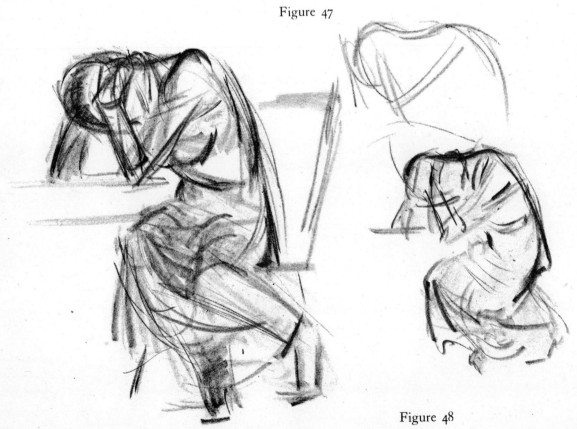

Figure 48

6: *Drawing for Children*

Several centuries ago a Chinese intellectual said, "Creation is a combination of vision and will. Vision gives the plan and will is the human energy that builds to completion."

Certainly the most valuable quality a child or adult possesses in relation to his future is his own individual personality and his ability to express himself in terms of his own "vision."

This vision or ability of perceiving life about one, individualistically and creatively, can be helped to grow and expand by intelligent, constructive appreciation of the child's effort and desire to express himself. It can be warped, and misdirected, and killed by wrong criticism through the desire of the parents or teachers to see the child make more "realistic" or completed pictures, or to have him "progress."

Charles Darwin once said, "If I had my life to live over again, I would make it a rule to read some poetry, listen to some music, and see some painting or drawing at least once every week, for perhaps the part of my brain now atrophied would then have been kept alive through life. The loss of these tastes is a loss of happiness."

Certainly happiness in living, in the sense Darwin intends above, and delight in freedom of doing are among the most worth-while experiences for children—vital stimuli to the successful future of our young people in their effort to learn, express, and expand. Therefore parents and teachers should be alert to recognize and encourage all talent or expressive desire in children. For that desire and talent can contribute enormously to their development as complete human beings. And this is true regardless of what each child will do in life, as Darwin the naturalist is witness.

Sympathetic appreciation together with sound understanding is absolutely essential to keep alive and to develop the child's talent and his desire for self-expression.

From the beginning of a young child's interest in expressing himself with drawing he should be encouraged and helped to come into contact with and to observe all the things and moods he can in the world about him: how clouds, sunsets, rainy days, storms affect the way nature looks, affect trees, streets, animals, people. Point these changes and moods out to him. He will soon realize that they happen, and he will then observe for himself and begin soon to be interested, more and more, in all that is happening around him that he can see. Don't try to encourage a child immediately to draw any of these observations; let the experience he has had grow in his mind, and soon enough he will be affected by it and will want to express his experience himself in some way with his pencil or crayon or brush.

There should be no limit to the contacts a child may experience in observation, in both country and city: the crowds of people in rain, in sunshine, at play and work; animal life; the sea; streams and rivers. Talk about them to the child, of the life, sadness, beauty, turmoil, freedom, joy. The child has a great interest in discovering all these things.

Do not attempt to explain how these things are made or should be drawn or how you think they look, only express how you feel about them, how they affected you. Then probably the child will realize that he too was affected in some way, and eventually he will do something about that affect and express it in his own way.

The greatest progress will be the result of perfect freedom of expression and thought. Encourage them constantly and do not be disturbed if the child doesn't think or see as you do or as you think he ought to. Let him find out for himself. The result will be a heightening of his creative interest and effort, intensified if you answer his questions whenever he asks them.

Generally speaking every child has a definite desire and talent to express himself in an individual (creative) way. Children dance, responding to the rhythm of music, or they listen quietly, or they sing. And children draw, scribbling shapes and colors with pencil and paper, or with any other tools they can find.

The desire to draw is natural to most children from the age of three on, and sometimes even earlier. But their talents are tremendously varied—it is impossible to judge how deep they run or how fine their quality. Judgments are meaningless. All that is important is to meet each child's expressive needs as he feels them, to help him by giving him the materials he wants, and the freedom to use them as he wants.

The child must be left perfectly free to choose his own subject and way of doing. Some children may like color best, others form, others texture. They may want to compose with any material from mud to French chalk. And yet a great many children have an urge to express themselves by making drawings with pencil or crayons on paper, not only because these materials are easily come by, but also for the simple reason that they most easily create a form or picture that describes and illustrates an object or experience that a child has known or would like to know about.

Drawing is one of the best mediums for a child to achieve a self-satisfactory result with during the earliest stages of his efforts of expression. He will also like to paint, with finger paints, poster paints, or water color. I believe this larger work gives him greater freedom of action in both mind and body which will develop his courage and confidence in tackling any inspirations or ideas he feels necessary to express. On the whole large sheets of paper, large brushes, and large crayons are best, as he may feel confined by small sheets of paper and as the larger tools are easier for him to handle. In this connection water colors are probably better at a somewhat later stage, being more difficult to manage, but he can learn to handle them with big brushes and paper around the ages of five or six.

I am convinced that however well or badly the young child succeeds in his effort to draw his chosen subject the result should *never* be criticized or corrected *except by himself*. Understanding and appreciation of his effort is vital. Encouragement and praise is most constructive. Time will develop his ability to say what he wants and say it well on paper.

If the child is not satisfied with the result of his efforts he will and should be the one to correct it by doing it over, or by drawing something else. A child's muscles are not sufficiently developed and co-ordinated for him to draw with great factual accuracy at an early age. As he grows older he will achieve greater control. At the same time it is natural that he has had little experience in life; he sees things as they are according to his own experience of them, and he draws with less detail and objectivity. Here too it is a matter of growth.

The most important motivations of a child's expressive efforts are his emotions. Let him freely express anything he feels in any way he chooses. As he grows and observes more he will unconsciously develop the ability to reveal his emotional reactions to his experiences.

Children can be too easily misguided and directed away from their own creative instinct by interested parents and teachers who think they know more and best. We know little or nothing of what a young child's reaction may be in relation to his experiences, much less do we understand how he feels about or should express himself in a drawing. Encourage the child to do more and more drawing. Always discourage all copying of other drawing. With my own children I have found that they respond fully to the reasoning that they were taking another artist's drawing when they copied and that they had no such right, that they didn't truly want to be like that other artist. Copying kills all self-reliance, creative desire, and individuality and shows no talent or ability that is worthy of praise.

As the child grows older he will have developed through his experiences a more definite desire and positive feeling of how he can best express himself and his desires. At this same time he may want to draw more accurately, but he must learn always to be his own critic, and he must be left free to rely completely on his own judgment. The child's progress and the development of his own creative individual personality depend entirely on the complete freedom he has had in expressing himself. With this complete freedom in thinking and drawing the young and older artist will seldom be at a loss for something vital and personal to say.

Time and experience will gradually and constructively gather the necessary facts. Practice and desire will gradually develop technical ability so the child will draw more correctly what he feels most vital and necessary to complete his idea, drawing or painting.

This should satisfy his family who have sympathetically and understandingly given him complete freedom.

The child's selection and interest in what he wants to draw have certainly a close connection to what his interests in his life are. If he is interested in horseback riding he will draw horses and all the things he thinks horses do and the things he would like to do with horses. If he rides in the country or lives in the country, he will most likely put in his drawings the kind of trees and country he would like to live in with his horses. Living these, he unconsciously observes them, and you will find he gets more beauty in his trees and country and hills. He will get the spirit of the horses, the hills, and the trees. The spirit is the strength and beauty of his drawing.

Girls generally love dolls and babies. They may therefore draw pictures of large families, queens, and princes. A girl may want to draw a mother hugging her baby. She may draw one arm much longer than the other in the effort to make the mother really hug her baby. The spirit of hugging is the important answer, not the correct length of the arm.

The child may draw great groups of children, playing, crying, laughing, running. The all-important story in the child's mind, effort, and picture is that spirit of the people doing or feeling these things. To recognize, appreciate, and encourage that effort and desire is the greatest help hopeful parents can give to their seemingly talented art-minded child.

From the age of fourteen and up children will very likely find other interests, such as swimming, dancing, tennis, football, etc. They may then entirely stop drawing or show very little interest in it. Their earlier interests and efforts in drawing were an indication of a desire to express themselves. They may find, through isolating themselves from drawing, that their true desires may be better expressed, as they learn to use words and read, in writing stories. Music, dancing, or acting may at this point become their preferred medium of self-expression. Their early work and freedom in drawing will be of great help—no matter what medium they may choose later for expression. I repeat, complete freedom of expression is the clearest direction and the only constructive way.

It is a fact that most people are born with very little or no creative artistic sense or talent. The urge and desire of an individual to draw, write, paint, etc., does by no means guarantee any creative quality or talent. And I have labored the point that art can be developed but not taught. Yet this is a happy thought. In the last analysis one's true, one's idiosyncratic worth is indifferent to the teachings of anyone.

It is true that the urge to draw or paint can be encouraged and directed to a very high degree of technical expression and knowledge, if the individual with the urge is willing and able to spend most of his time applying himself in that direction. One can be taught to draw, paint, write, or play a musical instrument just as anyone can be taught to read, figure, or build houses. The

53

student can be taught to use colors to paint still life, figures, landscape, and any subject he is interested in; to handle the medium and put down a likeness of this subject he wants to draw or paint with great freedom, sometimes daring, so that the result looks courageous and positive. He can be taught to do the finest details and most subtle tones in color, to draw accurately, to know anatomy, to know almost anything about painting or drawing there is to know, the same with writing and music. The ability to learn and record these facts in drawing, painting, music and writing can be very highly developed to a most pleasing degree. But what cannot be taught, fortunately or unfortunately, is the creative, expressive side of art. Most good teachers of drawing, painting, etc., can teach you what they know and have learned through years of experience and experiment with their medium, but when it comes to creative expression their way is only theirs and never yours, and your value as an artist ceases to exist if you accept their way. Great artists are born and their talents developed. And only the art that grows from the student's own understanding and evaluation of the truth is genuine and valuable. In this he is dependent on himself alone.

7: *Notes*

EXPRESSIVE LINE DRAWING

There must be no confusion in thinking about what is meant by a line drawing or a drawing in line in relation to the meaning of *expression* in line.

I am not interested in talking of line drawing as a pure black and white drawing to be done with pen and ink for reproduction.

The kind of line I want you to draw with and study the expressive value of and think about is the line that can express form, color, tone, emotion, rhythm, and third-dimensional depths, light, and shadow.

Your effort and desire to express and your feeling for all the above qualities are your only true guides in expressing yourself in line. This expressive line drawing practice will help you tremendously in learning to simplify your masses of design and masses of form, it will help you to keep from excessive overmodeling in your efforts to acquire form in your painting and drawing.

I am here reproducing expressive line drawings of several of the old and modern masters which I believe will illustrate to the student the great broad possibilities and uses of expressive line and its very great value as a medium of artistic expression.

I want to analyze one kind of very expressive line which may be one so-called continuous line, and can suggest form in light, shadow, and color. It may be wrongly called an outline of a form. This kind of line varies in intensity and delicacy from a sensitive tone to a dark strong color. It may range from one extreme to the other before the artist breaks its continuance, before the artist feels he has fully expressed the form in light, shadow, and color. This line value when felt and handled intelligently may seem at first to be just a simple outline of a form, but when fully understood it expresses and gives the feeling of a true turning of the form, or planes of the form, in one continuous interrelationship: it gives a feeling of the form continuing around to its other or unseen side, just as tonal or color modeling can do.

These Hans Holbein and Degas drawings illustrate very conclusively the beauty and value of this highly expressive, even emotional, line. This kind of line is most often used by artists who usually express themselves in paint and color and want to make a line drawing or study of a proposed painting. This line is not used to indicate a definite accent or outline: it is used to express the turning of a form or plane in light or color.

The highly intelligent and sensitive artist will use this line for expression unconsciously, for he is not as conscious of drawing in line as he is of searching out a certain value in form without using color (as in a preliminary drawing for a painting in color).

Study the many volumes of drawings by the great painters, which can be found in libraries.

A THOUGHT ABOUT SEEING AND UNDERSTANDING OTHER ARTISTS' WORK

Whenever possible analyze and study the works of other artists. Go to all exhibitions and look at each picture with all of your artistic intelligence. Make every effort to study reproductions of all the modern and old masters' works in drawing, painting, and sculpture.

Your greatest effort must be in trying to appreciate the point of view and intention of each individual artist in his work. It is very important to take the same attitude toward the work of another artist that you would take toward the artist himself, or to any person you might meet and want to know. Your natural desire should always be for friendship, and for thorough understanding of the artist's personality and his personal point of view toward his work, his art, and its relation to life. After earnestly studying for this understanding, you can feel qualified to criticize, like and admire, pull apart, or completely disagree with the artist's work or point of view. You should, however, always be tolerant: another artist's sincerity of effort must be respected at all times. His point of view is right and somewhat satisfying to him just as yours is right for you. Understanding and artistic intelligence must be your guide.

To understand *why* you disagree and dislike is as important as to understand why you like and agree with another's point of view and work. To be destructively critical and disappointed in another artist's work before thoroughly studying it will only close your mind prematurely, block and destroy your chances of broader understanding and true appreciation. What each artist feels and what he thinks most important in his manner of expressing himself is entirely his own business. If you will learn to appreciate and understand what he is doing or trying to do, your own artistic experience will be greatly broadened.

MATERIALS—TOOLS TO WORK WITH

Whenever possible use the best materials to work with, especially brushes—both water color and oil—and pencils and crayons, for it is hard even with the finest tools to make your best work what you desire. Good artists would never think of trying to express themselves with anything but what they consider the very best equipment. With brushes, too, the best will far outlast poor or cheap ones if good care is taken of them and they are washed and cleaned thoroughly after being used.

Learn to work with many different mediums: pencil, charcoal, crayons of all kinds, water-color brush, India ink, etc. Select the medium that you think will best help you express what you are working for at the time.

The easiest mediums to handle are probably soft pencil, crayon, and charcoal, for they can be more easily corrected if it is necessary.

Try all kinds of available paper: a particular texture, which accepts one medium better than another, can help your effort tremendously.

Black ink with a good springy water-color brush is an excellent medium, as it forces you to work directly and with confidence.

In selecting your water-color brushes, look them over carefully and try them in water to be sure that when very wet they spring directly back after each stroke to the straight position they had when dry. Get a sabel brush with a sharp point, either red or black. Camel's hair is cheap and worthless. Sabel may seem expensive but it will wear and hold its shape for years. A good pliable springy sabel brush is a very sensitive instrument and well handled can do much to help you develop a more sensitive touch and directness in effort.

Pencil is always good for quick notes in your emergency pocket sketch book. Use the softer leads: B3, B4, B5.

In charcoal, the compressed (Russian) is very good. At least get a smooth stick charcoal that is soft.

Lithograph crayons must be tried, for they have a very fine value on most papers and are especially good for working out compositions. Whenever possible get the square sticks.

As for paper, all kinds are useful, but they must be tried. The cheapest kinds are very good for studies and sketches. By the time you are ready to make more advanced drawings, you will have found the kind of paper you think best for the answer you want. Naturally very absorbent papers are not best for water color or brush and ink work. Regular typewriter paper is perfectly good for sketching and study. Large blocks of regular new paper are obtainable and are fine for the same purpose. Charcoal takes a paper with more wash.

For water colors, you must use a paper made to take water color and moisture; otherwise you will be tremendously handicapped by too absorbent paper.

Use either art gum or kneaded rubber for erasures. The latter leaves no crumbs which often is a great advantage, particularly with charcoal. It can also be kneaded to a useful sharp point or edge in the palms of your hands, if your hands are warm.

Practice drawing with as little use of the eraser as possible, in order to train yourself to sureness of purpose, directness, and confidence in the result of your efforts. It is better to correct by drawing over an error, or making a new start, since the purpose of your drawings is research and exercise in thought and expression, rather than correct complete drawing as such.

Buy the same water colors and oils that professional artists use. Water colors in either tubes or jars are preferable. All oil colors come in tubes.

Keep your materials clean and in the best possible condition at all times in order not to be unnecessarily handicapped.

RICO LEBRUN, *This Is War*

Rico Lebrun's drawings are tremendously skillful and show great artistic force, once the artist decides what he wants to express with his model, whether in design, form, or emotion. Although his drawings are usually done directly from a model, they never seem to be so because he uses his model as a guiding reference, and at all times escapes a commonplace factual result. Some of his preparatory drawings are life size or larger.

There is definite emotional value in the drawing of a man kneeling (*This Is War*), as well as strong three-dimensional feeling and positive design, all executed in delicate line relating to form in light and shadow.

In the figure of *Woman in Dust Storm* (Frontispiece), Lebrun has obviously searched for, and successfully realized, great power of form, design, and expressive action.

59

RICO LEBRUN, *Dust Storm at 12*

Lebrun has also made a powerful study of form, design, and emotion in the direct
line treatment of the figure with arms spread (*Dust Storm at 12*). Note the importance
he has attached to the expression of the hands.

RICO LEBRUN, *Portrait of Anna*

This drawing, which was made to be used in a large mural fresco, has a very beautiful and powerful sense of form in a definite design. The artist has purposely used line to designate form rather than emotional quality.

Rico Lebrun is a young American artist and a truly great draughtsman of his time.

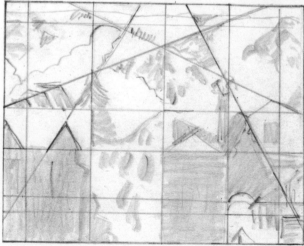

PRESTON DICKINSON, *Winter*

In this charcoal drawing, Preston Dickinson succeeded in working out a semi-abstract design of a realistic scene—snow covering hills, buildings, and trees. He did this by selecting certain lines of the buildings (shapes, edges, and tones), of the trees, and of the hill shapes, and without any obvious linear plane form he has created a three-dimensional space (see diagram). The diagram is an analysis of the design, emphasizing the frame-work.

Notice, too, how intelligently Dickinson has co-ordinated the details into his general design; the definite sense of the textures of snow, trees, hills, and buildings; and the fine variety of forms.

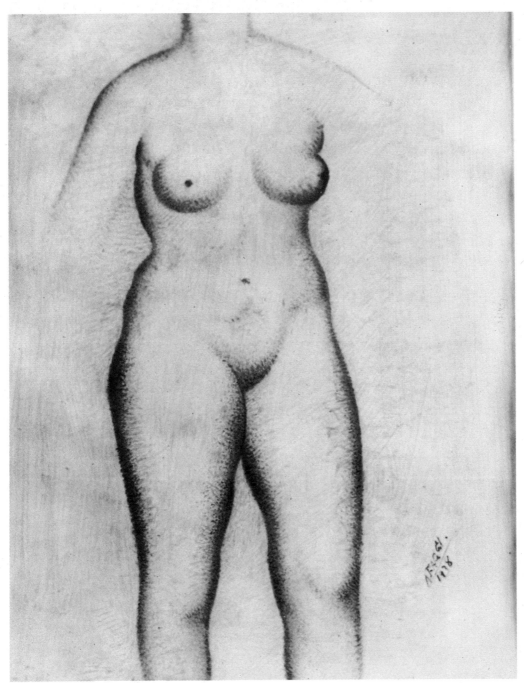

ALFEO FAGGI, *Nude*

   The entire form in this drawing by Alfeo Faggi, the sculptor, has a true plastic vitality running through it. The technique of fusing delicate, pliant parts to build a strongly co-ordinated bulk produces the lovely texture and design.

63

KAETHE KOLLWITZ, *The Unemployed*

The tragic hopelessness of unemployment to the breadwinner of a family is fully expressed in this emotionally motivated drawing. The dragging of form and lines and the confused and lost facial expression make this an exceptionally moving drawing, therefore a very successful one as far as the all-important artist's direction is concerned.

From the Collection of Herman Shulman, New York. Courtesy of the Buchholz Gallery

KAETHE KOLLWITZ, *Mother with Two Children*

Here the artist has been primarily moved to express intense mother love and protective instinct. The general enveloping design and interrelation of the forms intensify this theme, as do the entwining arms and the head forms and expressions.

Ar. Guérinet, Editeur, Faubourg Saint-Martin 140, Paris

INGRES, *La Famille Gatteaux*

This Ingres drawing illustrates drawing as an end in itself. It is so complete that there is seemingly no more to be said about the subject. It fully explains itself and its use, as it displays the artist's knowledge and ability. There is a masterful organization of relative forms and lines: it is pure likeness well and thoroughly executed.

66

Uffizi Gallery, Florence

GENTILE BELLINI, *Study of a Man*

This study of drapery on form by a fifteenth-century Venetian painter is a fine explanatory drawing. At the same time that the artist is searching for the cause and effect of stress and strain of form on drapery, he uses the drapery to create the three-dimensional bulk, and the whole has a decidedly decorative quality. The careful selection of folds for their potential meaning produces an exquisite simplicity. Study the organization and analyze its decorative composition.

67

DEGAS, *Study for Portrait of Manet*

This Degas drawing shows the artist's fine understanding of and sensitive feeling for the value of pure line. Notice how he has created a definite feeling of bulk by very delicate lines, particularly in the head, the coat, and the arm within the sleeve. It is very important to study carefully this type of expressive line, which suggests form as it varies from light to heavy tones, often nearly breaking but coming back to pick up the moving form. Especially in the arm there is tremendous variety in the quality of line.

DEGAS, *Portrait of Emil Duranty*

In the head and hands of this study for a portrait there is a positive desire on the part of the artist to understand the true character and portray the likeness and personality of this individual. The body and arms are held to an almost flat surface, but the form is indicated in outline by a slight change of line value.

Degas has used a white chalk on the head and hands more fully to develop the form.

DEGAS, *Two Dancers*

Degas's main direction here is for an effect of light and shadow, held together in a simple decorative manner. At the same time there is a positive feeling of solid form in space.

DEGAS, *Seated Violinist*

This drawing was made for emotional expression, and the outline drawing of the tonal patterns was definitely of great importance to the artist at the time.

MATISSE, *Girl in Rumanian Blouse*

In making this drawing, Matisse has used a pen-and-ink outline method which best expresses the decorative simplicity in the design of the figure in the blouse. Matisse has also created a convincing three-dimensional feeling by the interrelation and breaking of this pure black line and by the suggestion of the plane positions of the decorative linear shapes.

From the Collection of John S. Newberry, Jr., Grosse Pointe Farms, Michigan. Courtesy of the Museum of Modern Art

MATISSE, Study for *White Plumes*

Matisse made a number of sketches for the final painting of *White Plumes*. These pure line drawings clearly show his desire to search out all possibilities of his subject. They are drawn in pencil and show a very sensitive touch and feeling for pure line. Matisse always has a strong decorative direction. but there is also a definite three-dimensional value.

CÉZANNE, *Boy Writing*

This simple *direct* sketch by Cézanne of a boy writing was inspired by the artist's desire to record especially the intention in the boy's concentration as he writes. He instinctively drew lines and forms that express not only the intention of the boy but also Cézanne's own vital interest in the use of these abstract lines and forms as an organization. As a result, he eliminated all unnecessary and useless forms, which would only illustrate facts and get in the way of the expressive and emotional value of the meaning he wishes to convey.

HANS HOLBEIN, *Drawing of a Woman*

This Holbein drawing illustrates well the meaning of sensitive, expressive line, by
the use of which he has created a flesh-and-blood character and a solid, three-dimensional
head and figure in a most beautiful and decorative manner. The delicate line of the face
and features gives the feeling of the interrelation of forms and planes which move around
the whole form of the woman. What might be termed an outline is actually a sensitively
drawn form expressed in delicate line by a highly perceptive master.

JEROME MYERS, *Street Shrine*

Jerome Myers' great interest was in people—how they lived, what they did and thought about life and in what surroundings, their emotions and how they were affected by them. This drawing is worked out from notes and observations of characters on the spot, in this case an altar. It is possible too that the whole drawing was completed on the spot in one sketch.

JEROME MYERS, *The Old Philosopher*

This quick sketch (or note of characters plus a note of emotion) of a group of
figures against a background is the kind of observation to be made in your pocket sketch
book, at the time of observation if possible. It is the kind of sketch, too, which can be
made from notes taken on the spot, put together while fresh in your mind as a future
reference note of experience. This is an excellent drawing because it records a true note
of an experience that was of importance to the artist, and it undoubtedly proved valuable
to Jerome Myers as a reminder of what vitally interested him at a given moment.

77

Courtesy of the Art Institute of Chicago. Gift of Mr. and Mrs. Wm. N. Eisendrath

ARISTIDE MAILLOL, *Reclining Nude*

This study drawing is a fine example of a sculptor's search for the beauty of pure form and simplicity of design. The sculptor is naturally conscious of form primarily, and what he can do with it in his particular manner of expression. He is always working with three-dimensional solids and consequently must consider his design from all points of observation. A sculptor's drawing therefore, as in *Reclining Nude,* is dominated by a consciousness of bulk and space.

ANTON REFREGIER, *Grief*

The artist in making this drawing was inspired by a desire to express a pure emotion, motivated by hearing some of the first tragic news of the Spanish War over the radio. His wife at the time was sitting at a table reading a newspaper which was spread out before her. The news so affected them both that her very position communicated tragedy to Refregier, and he immediately made this and several other sketches.

Anton Refregier is an important mural painter. Instinctively, therefore, he has arrived at a design of three-dimensional value with real emotional intent.

Photo Druet

Photo Druet

RENOIR, Studies for *Les Grandes Baigneuses*

These studies of Renoir's are of great value and interest to the student because they show clearly Renoir's vital desire and intention in his search for the most important values in the building up of a composition, and also the uses of the various unities he wanted in the final painting.

The more roughly done drawing was made to register the composition as a whole, and shows an effort to suggest the space and relative direction of the background to the

grouping of figures. In the upper left hand corner Renoir has even noted the type of design he felt would be most suitable to frame the finished picture.

In the other drawings he is searching further for the finer design, for the best positions and emotional expressions of the separate figures. This is shown particularly well in the figure which belongs in the lower right hand corner of the composition, in the delicate turn of the head, the line of the back, the position of the arms and hands, all of which are of great value in directing Renoir to his final goal.

81

From the Phillips Memorial Gallery, Washington, D.C. Courtesy of the Museum of Modern Art

RENOIR, Study for *The Judgment of Paris*

In this study by Renoir for his painting *The Judgment of Paris* he seems to be mainly exploring in an effort to create a moving, living three-dimensional space by means of a grouping and relative placing of several figures. The accent on forms with heavier lines and tones combines and holds together the four figures in one three-dimensional mass. At the same time, this varied, sensitive line causes an effect of life and emotion within the group, which exists in light and shadow as well as in an organized mass.

82

LEONARDO DA VINCI, *Sheet of Sketches for Madonna*

Here Leonardo da Vinci has made a number of drawings in search of a design in the grouping of figures and drapery that will help express an emotional urge and message that the artist felt was all vital and essential to his final expressive desire. These research drawings are preliminary studies for a part of a finished painting.

Study the use of drapery to create design of form and rhythmical and emotional organization of the unit. Note also the simplicity of the emotional action and attitude of the figures and the effort to make the whole co-ordinate.

83

REMBRANDT, *Study for Pieta*

These sketches were made purely for some emotional expression desired by the artist, which eventually he used for reference in making a final picture. They have the feeling and freedom of writing, although Rembrandt's direction is positive.

REMBRANDT, *Women Reading* and *Two Studies of a Woman*

In these quick sketches there is not only great freedom from fact finding but also the notable directness of Rembrandt's desire to find out and put down only what was vital and necessary to him in expressing the emotional intention or important form of the subjects. The woman reading illustrates that intention well. There is a suggestion of form and of light and shadow effects, although the woman reading and a general design of organization is of more vital importance.

In the two other pen-and-ink drawings Rembrandt is looking for a simple way of creating a form which exists as a bulk in light and shadow.

EUGENE SPEICHER, *Head of a Peasant*

Courtesy of the Artist

REMBRANDT, *The Death of the Virgin* (1639)

In this etching, *The Death of the Virgin,* Rembrandt has expressed the meaning of every quality of line in drawing with the greatness of a master's power and understanding. One must analyze the etching thoroughly, from many angles and for many different reasons, in order to appreciate the various values and uses the artist has made of his line, and the consequent power with which he has expressed emotion, drama, space, light, concave and convex form, color, tonal delicacy and contrast, design in pattern, design in light and shadow, and the meaning and use of drapery and texture—all vigorously organized into one powerful emotional composition with one direction.

Study thoroughly, too, the emotional and dramatic meaning of each individual figure: in the pose and the expression of face, hands, and arms in response to the death of the Virgin, which was the dominating direction of Rembrandt's effort in this etching (drawing). These qualities are all expressed by the weight and delicacy of touch and by direction of line. The artist's touch was guided entirely by his desire to express something about which he felt a decided emotion, never once forgetting the power of organization or the meaning of direction.

Study each figure for its own individual beauty of drapery, design, form, and for its meaning in the emotional drama. Search out the reason for and use of each figure, each mass of tonal value, and the direction and rhythm of form and line in the action. relative to the over-all composition.

86

Courtesy of the Metropolitan Museum of Art

Courtesy of the Corcoran Gallery of Art, Washington, D.C.

Courtesy of the Addison Galley of American Ar
Andover Art Studio Photograph

EUGENE SPEICHER, *Red Moore* (1), (2)

These are two of several drawings made by the artist in preparation for a large full figure canvas of Red Moore. In the first one his search for character and form is very evident, and the whole is strongly held together by definite relative direction of lines and planes, especially in the build and design of the head in relation to the neck, shoulders, and chest. In the other drawing Speicher has made a definite search for the character of the relative moving forms and planes as a solid three-dimensional bulk.

INVENTORY '80